This Coloring Book Belongs To :

KIDS 4--9

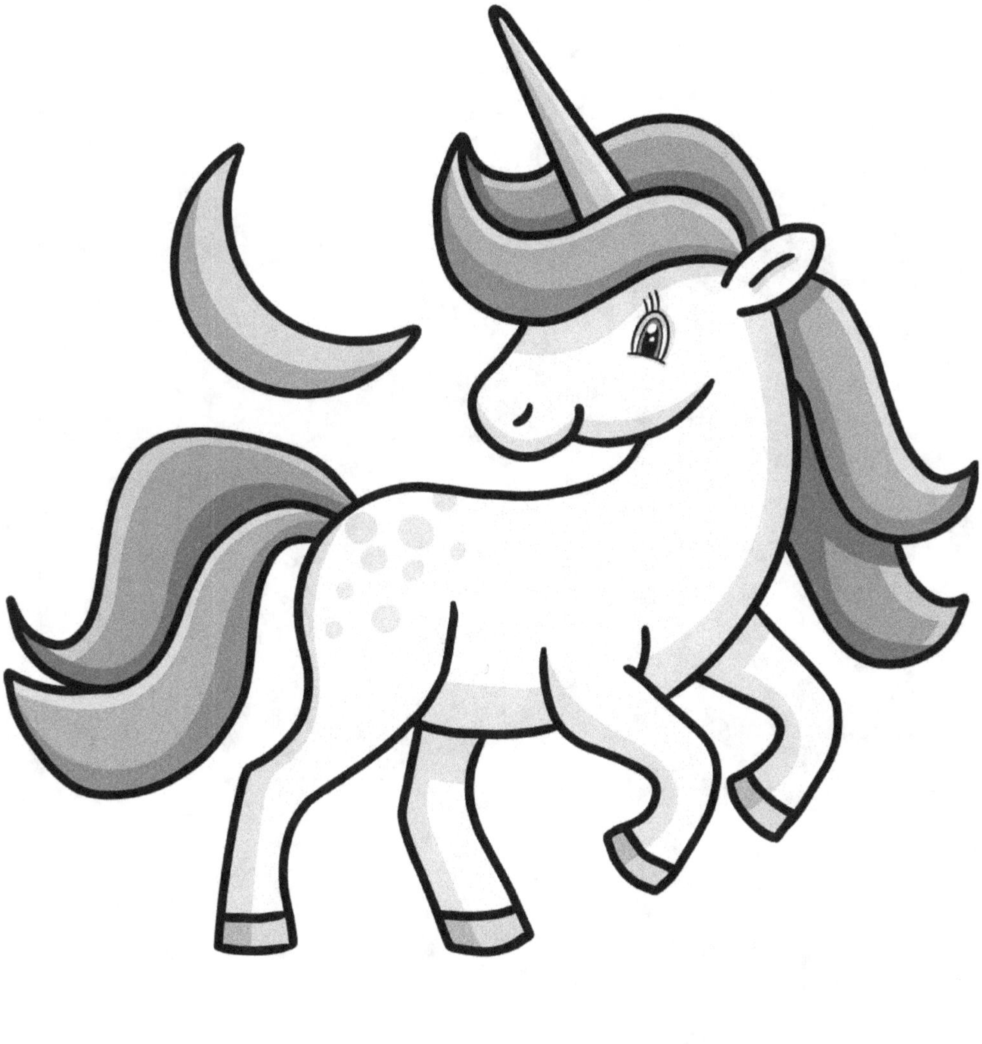

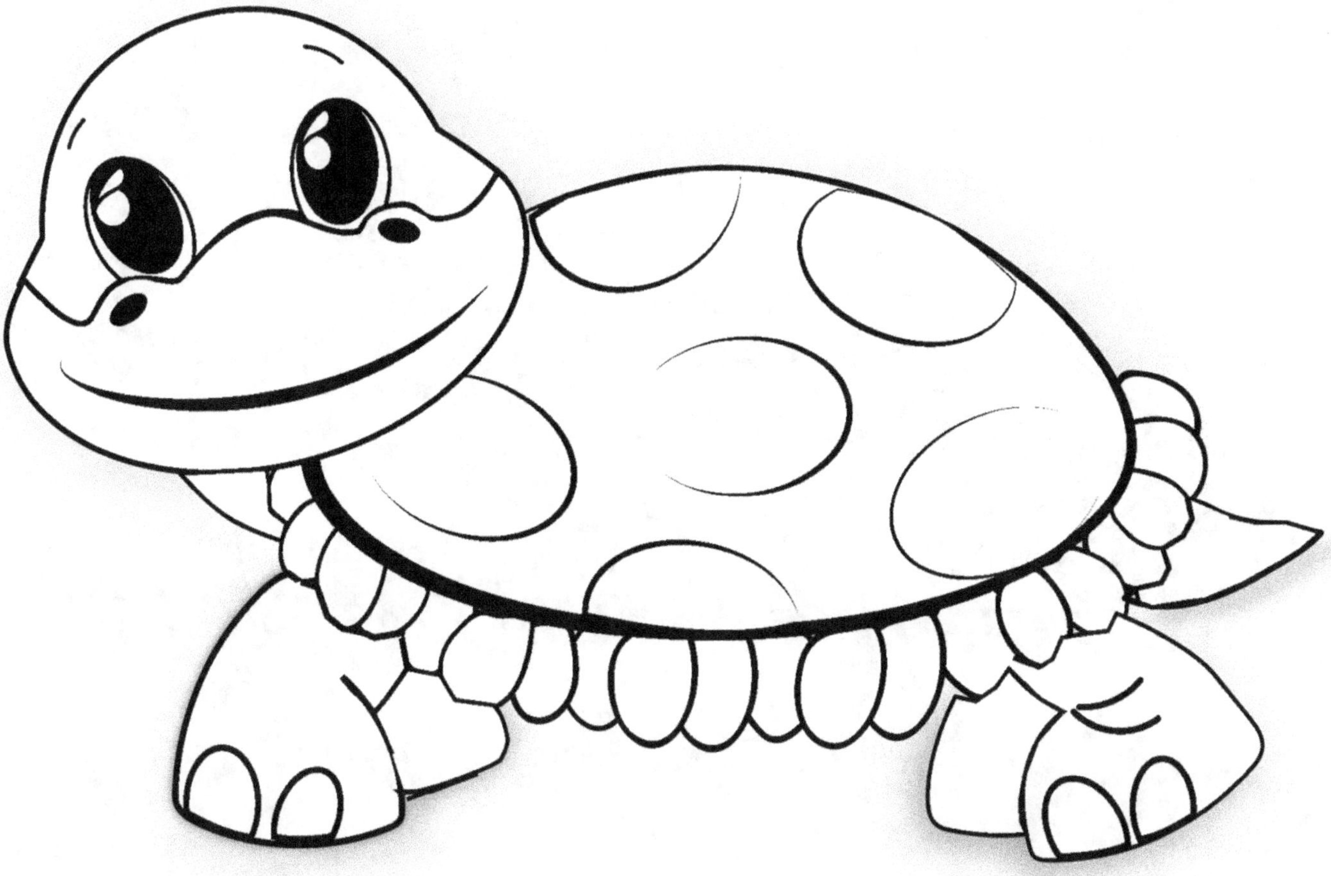

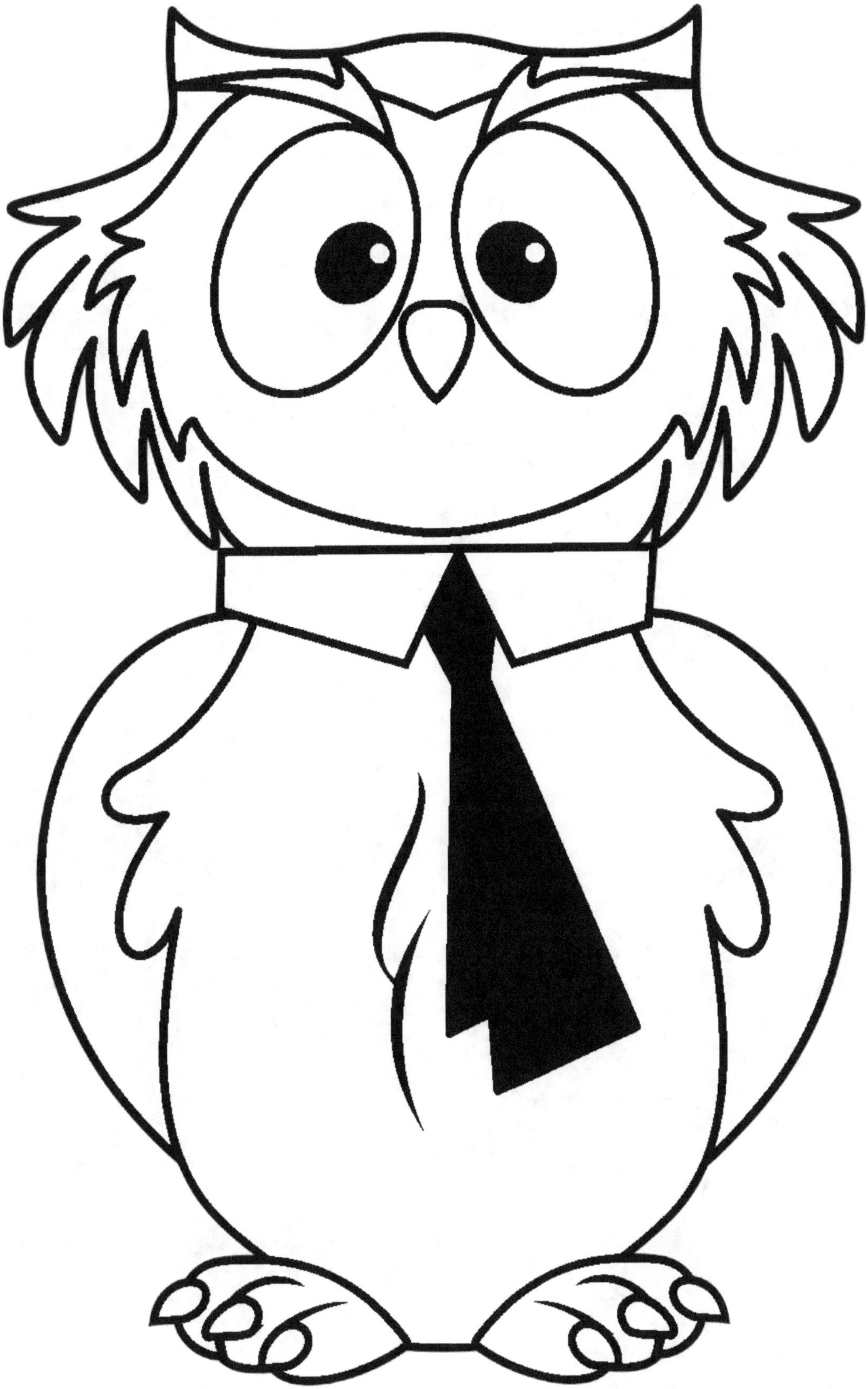

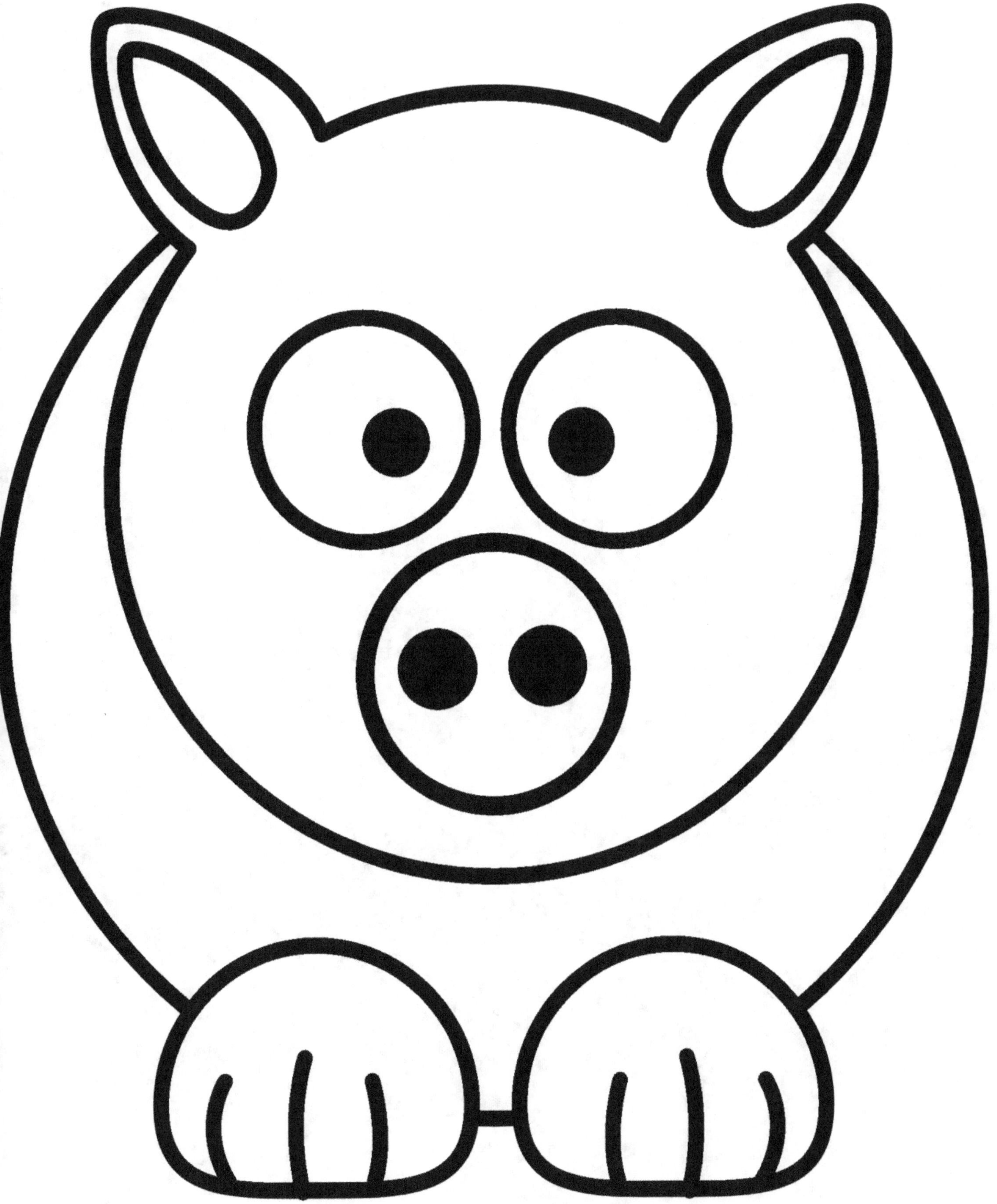

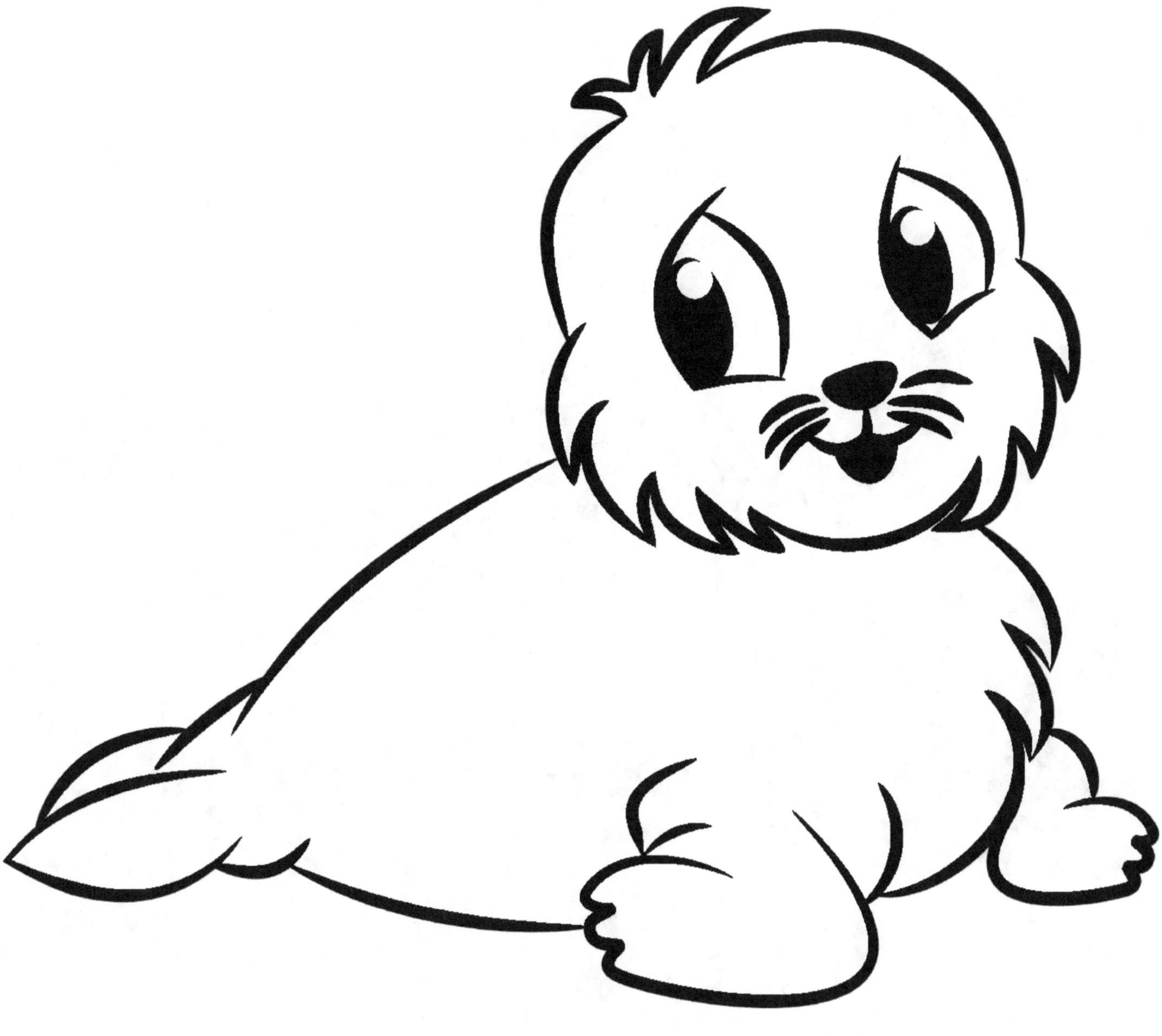

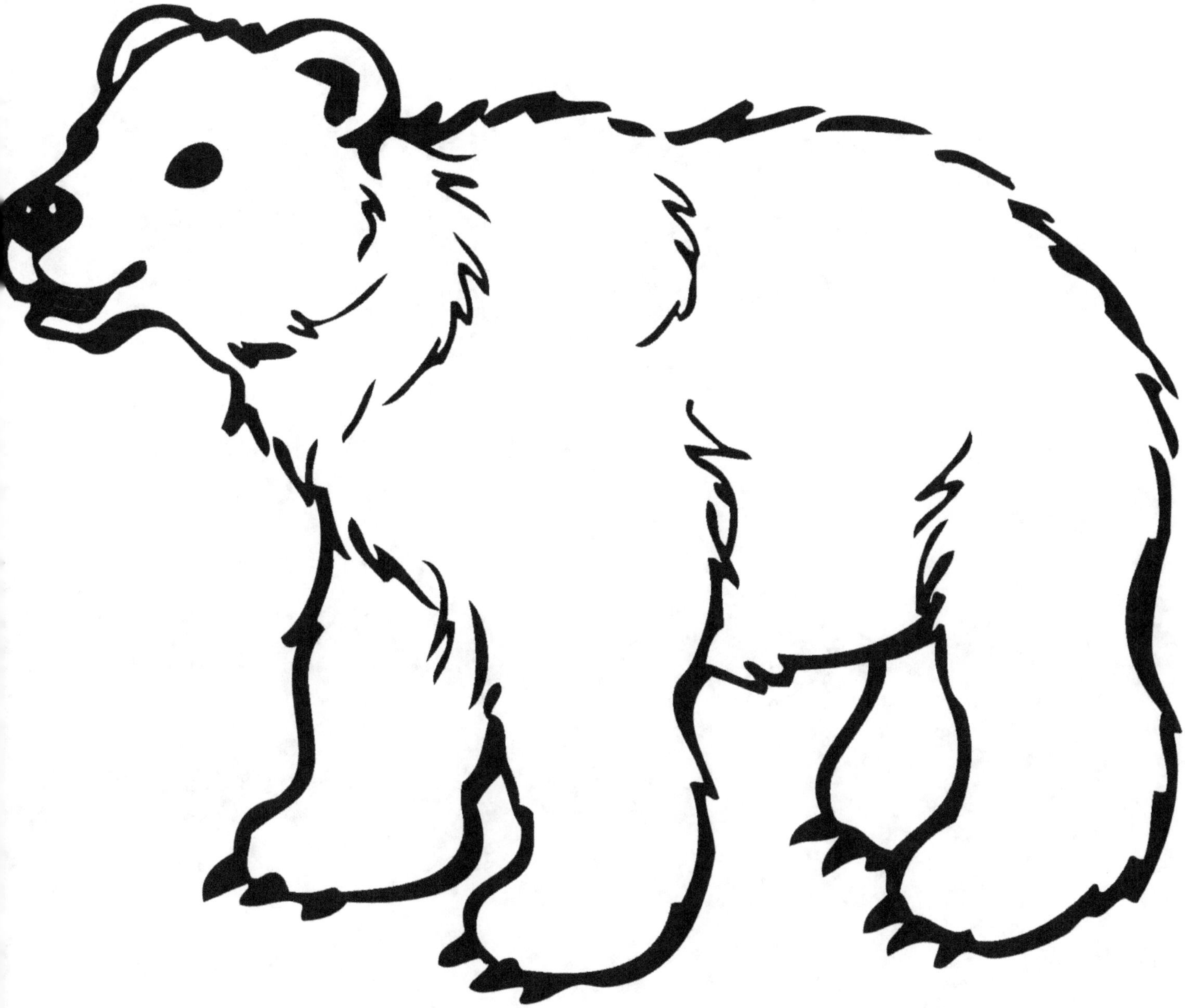

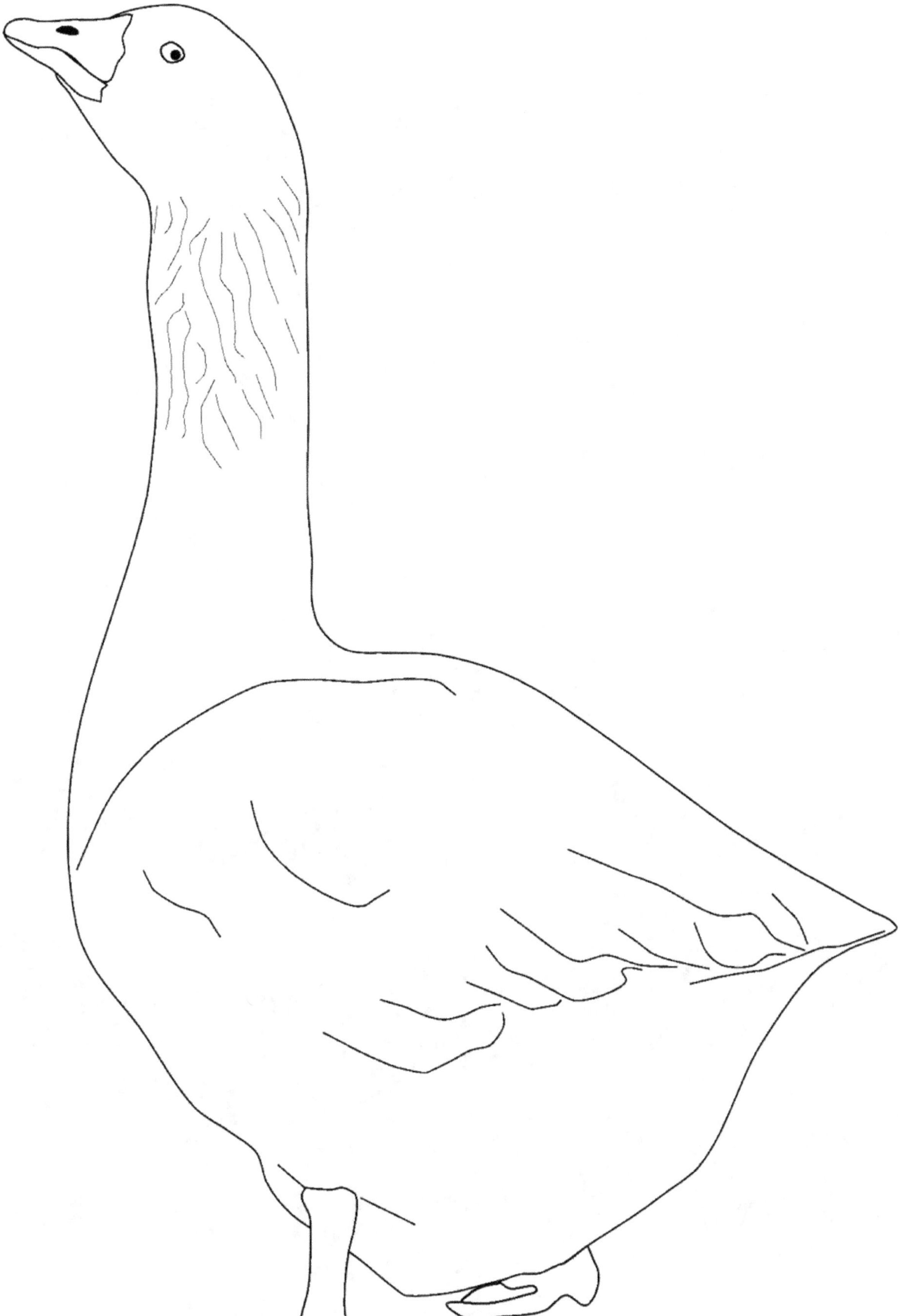

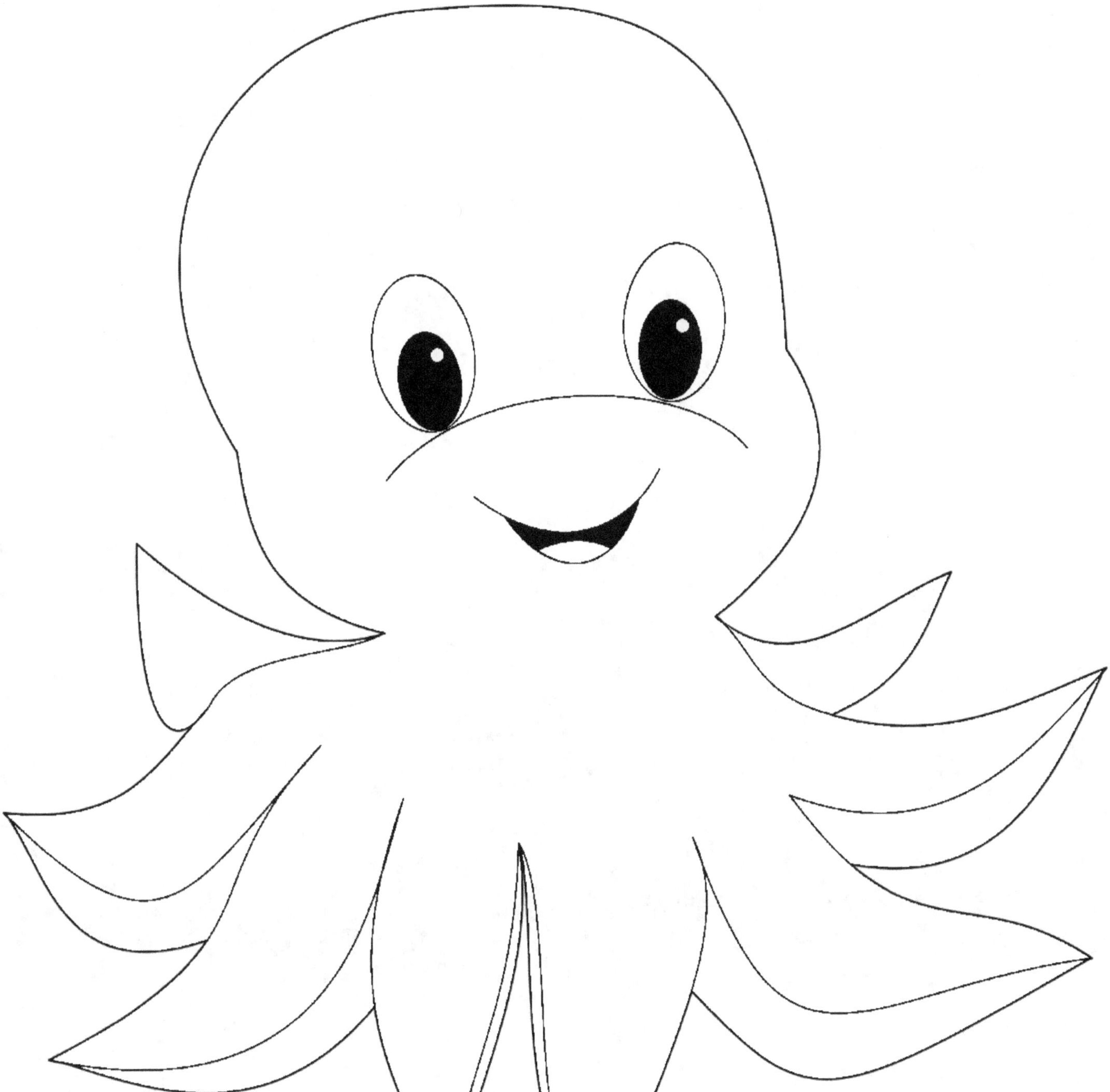

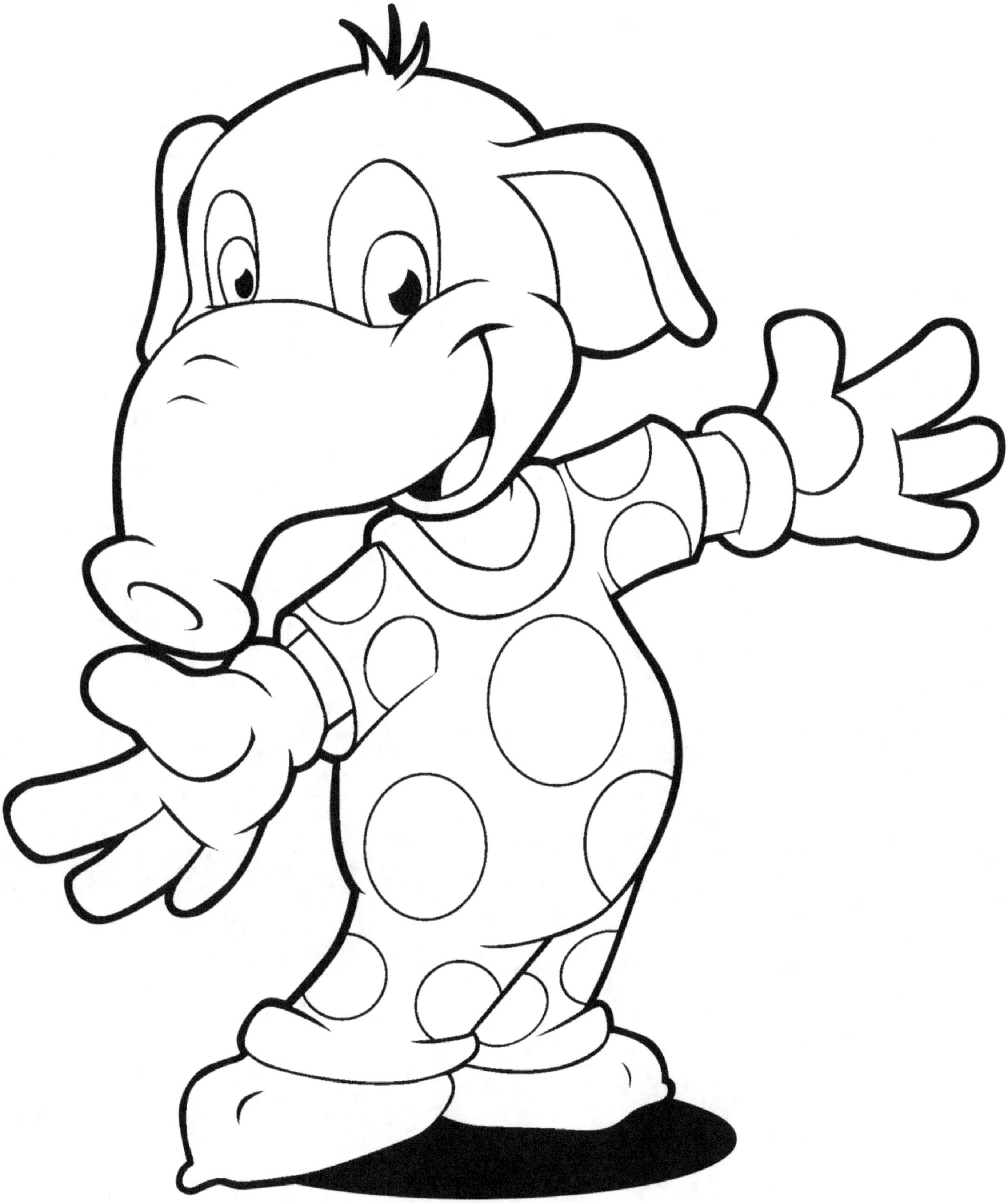

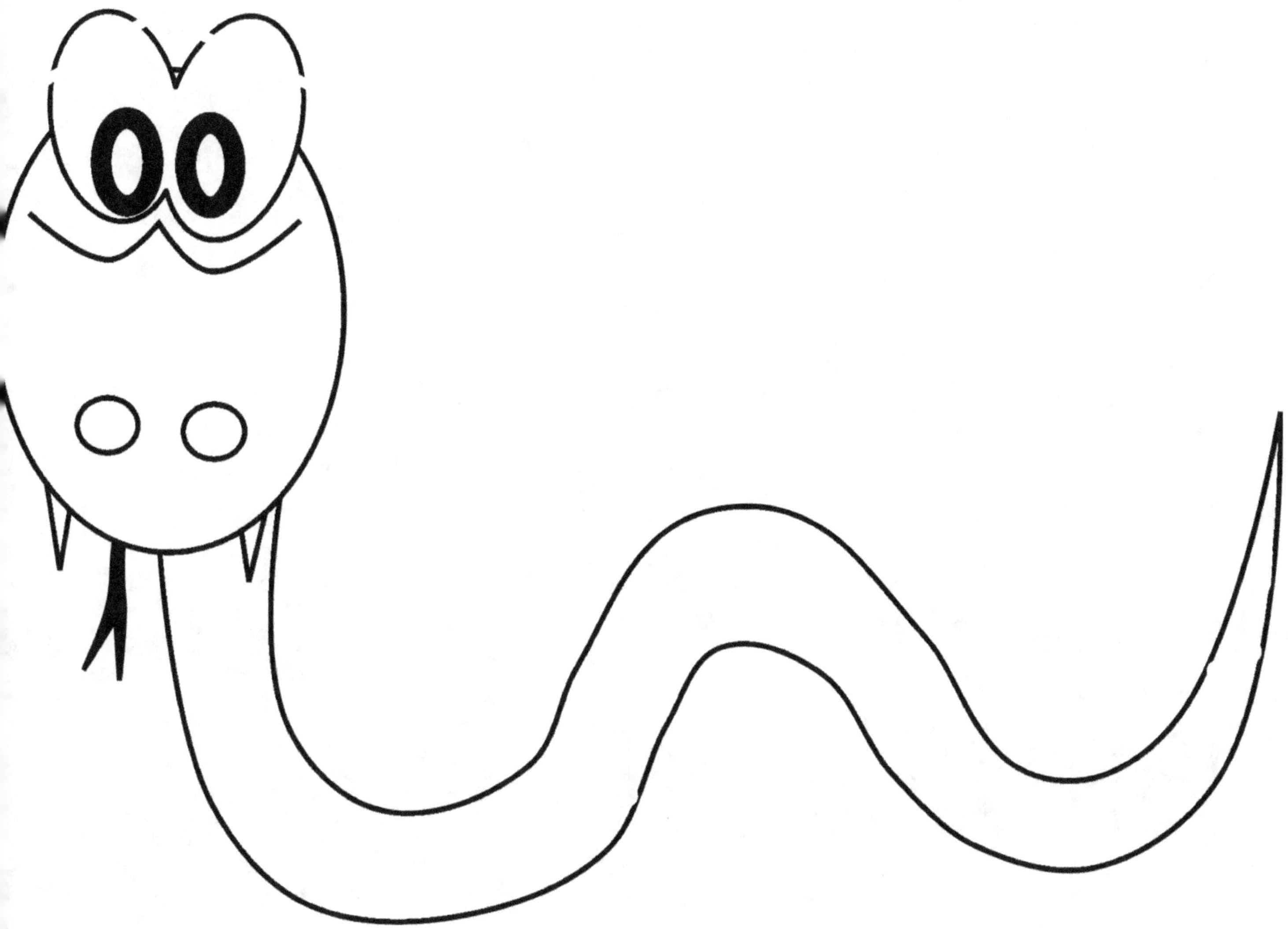

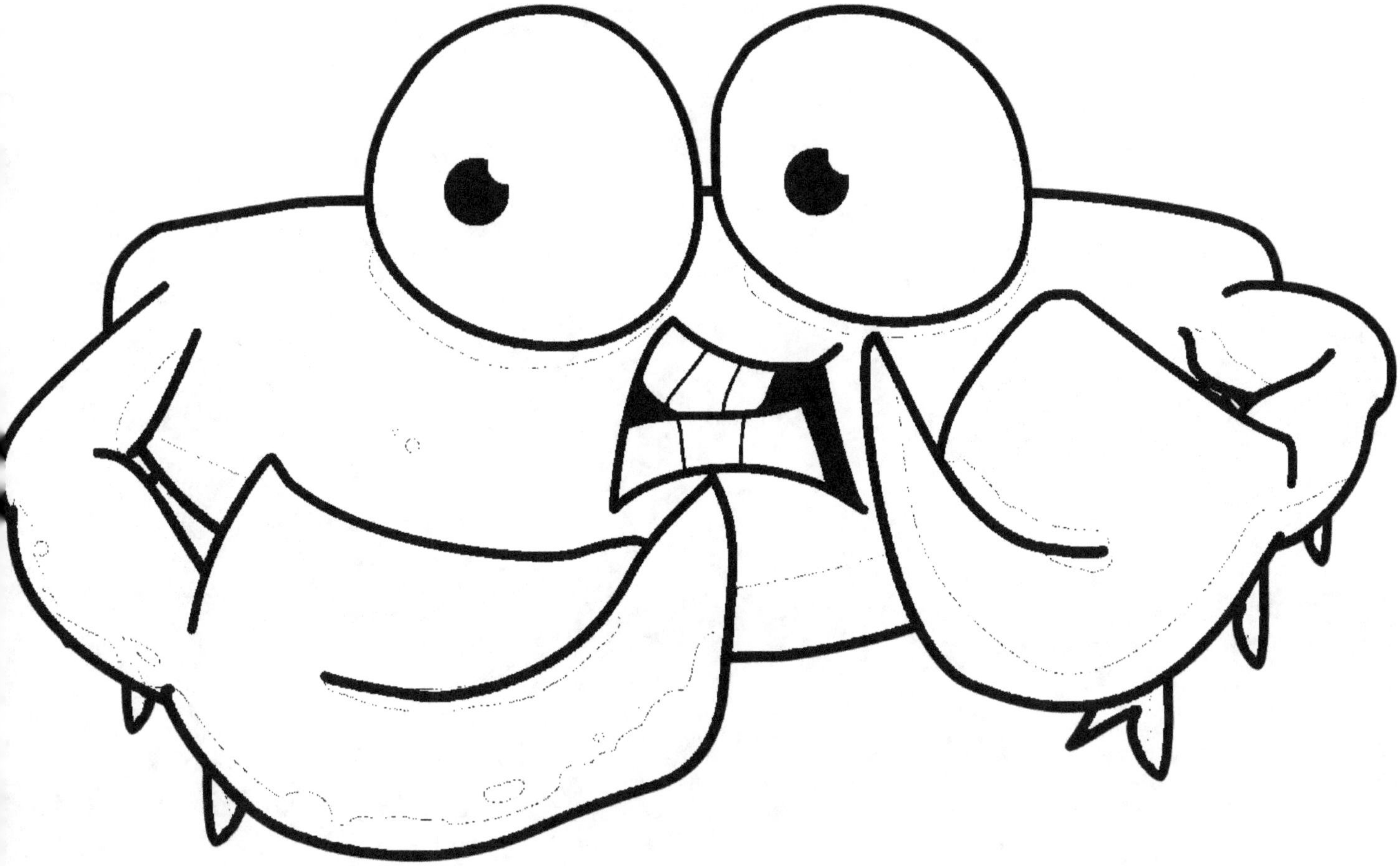

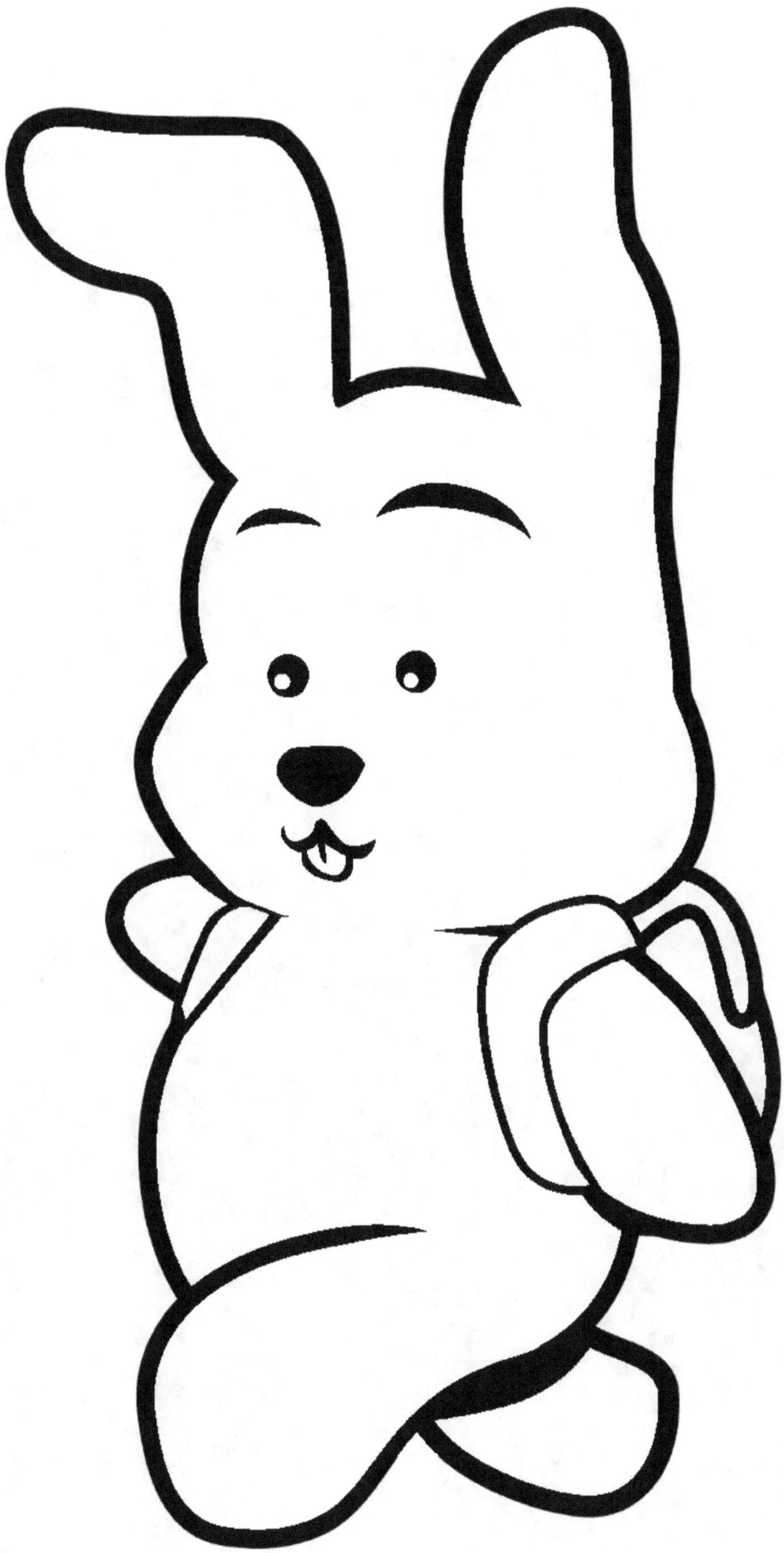

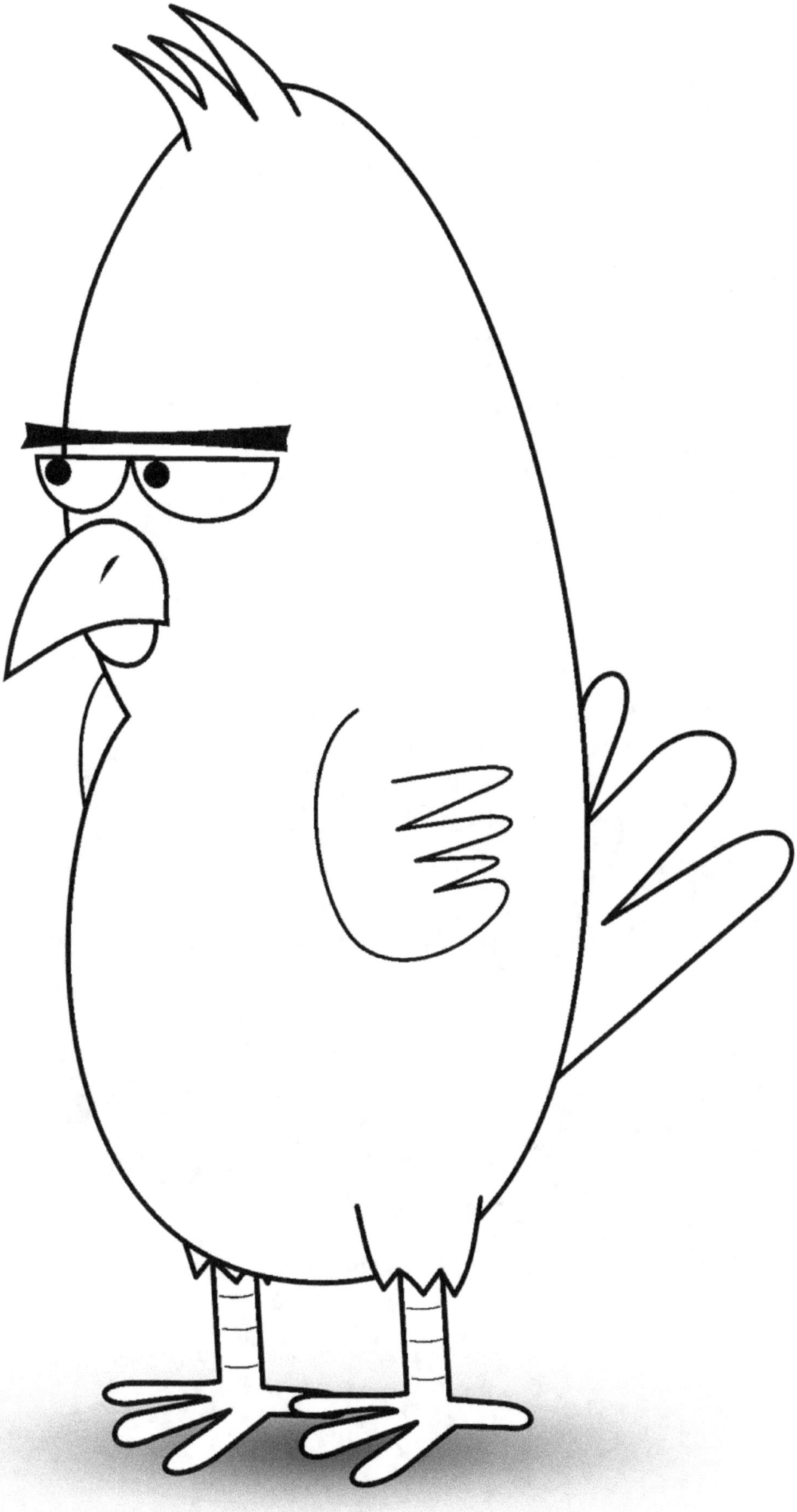

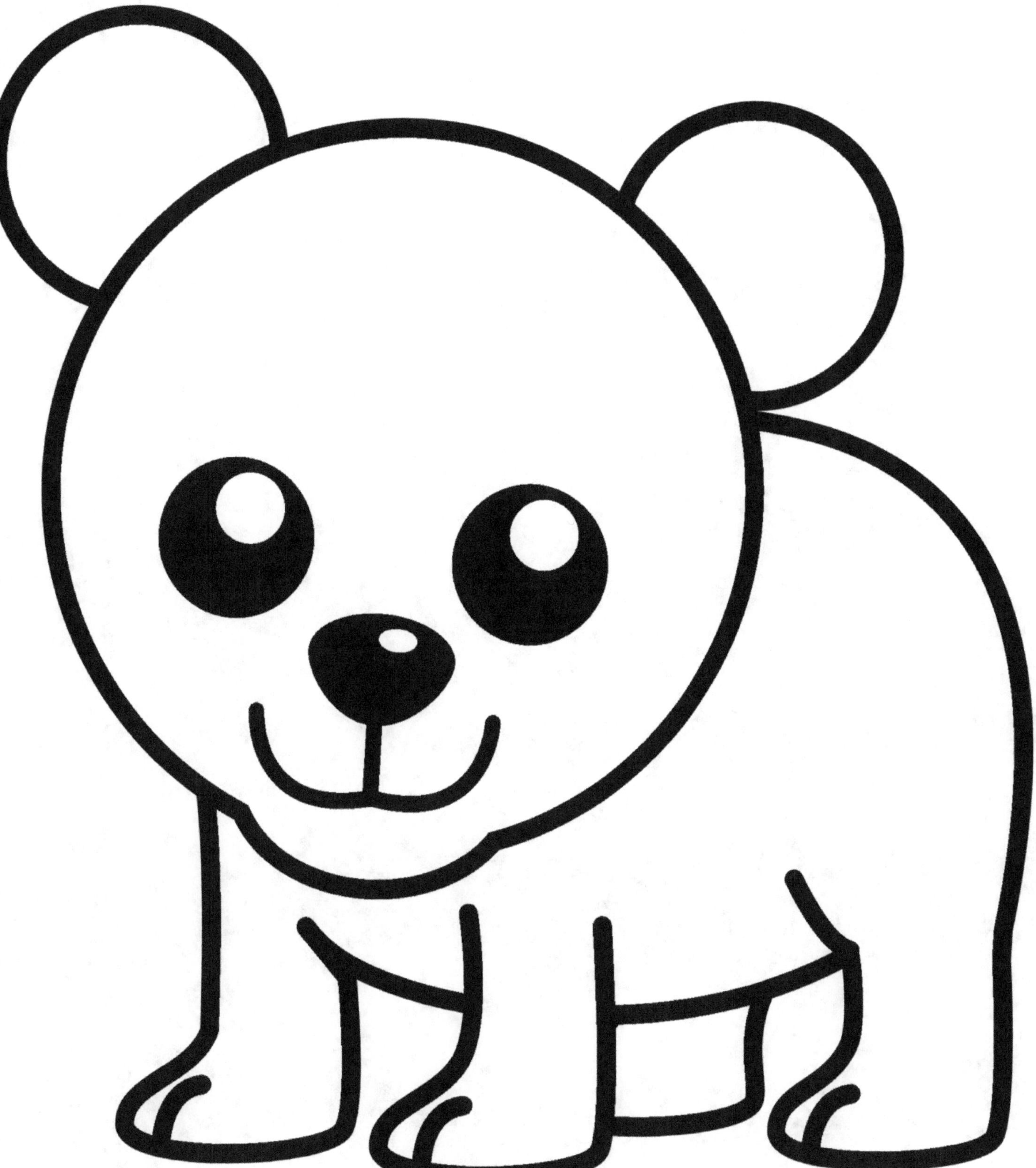

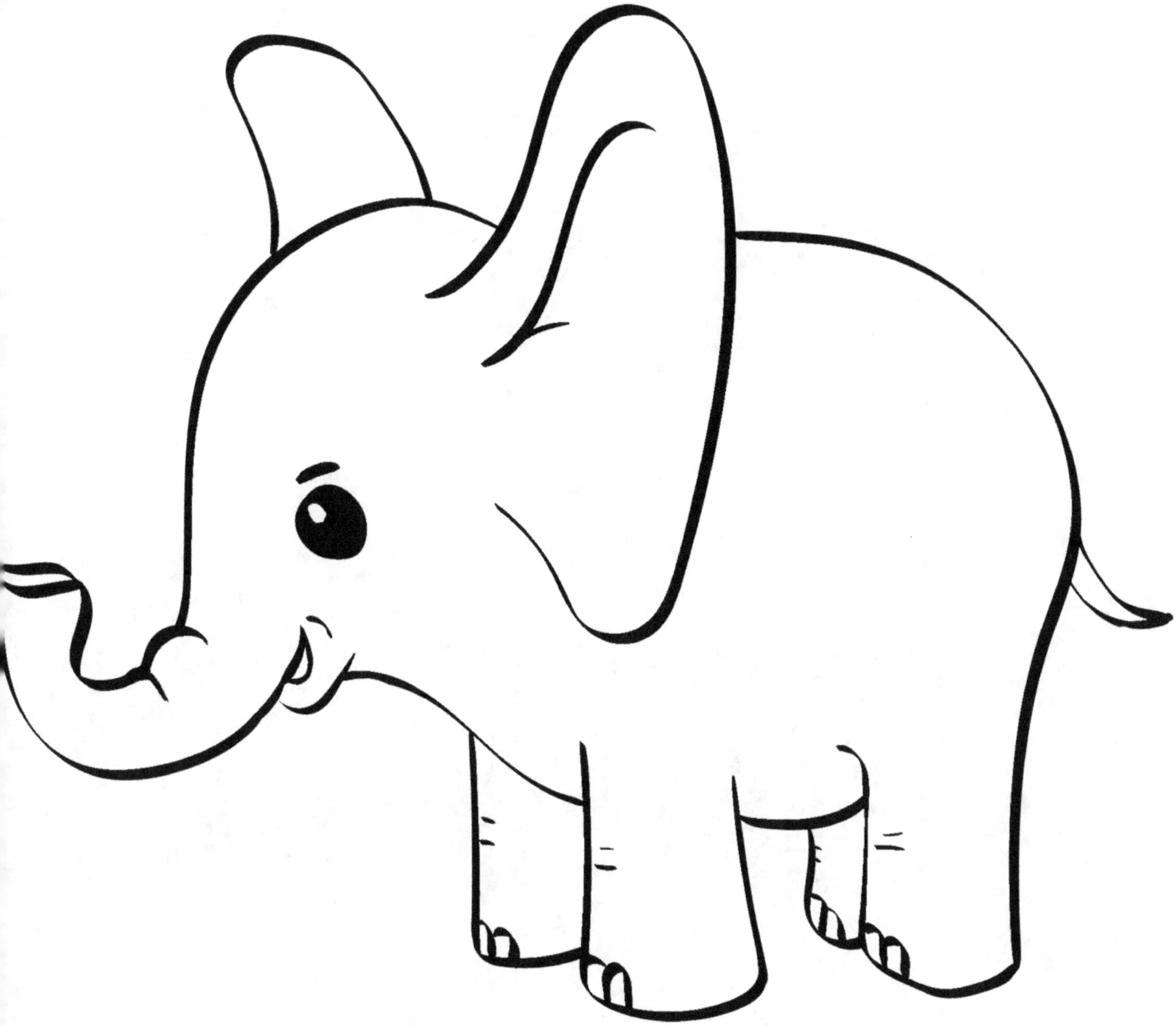

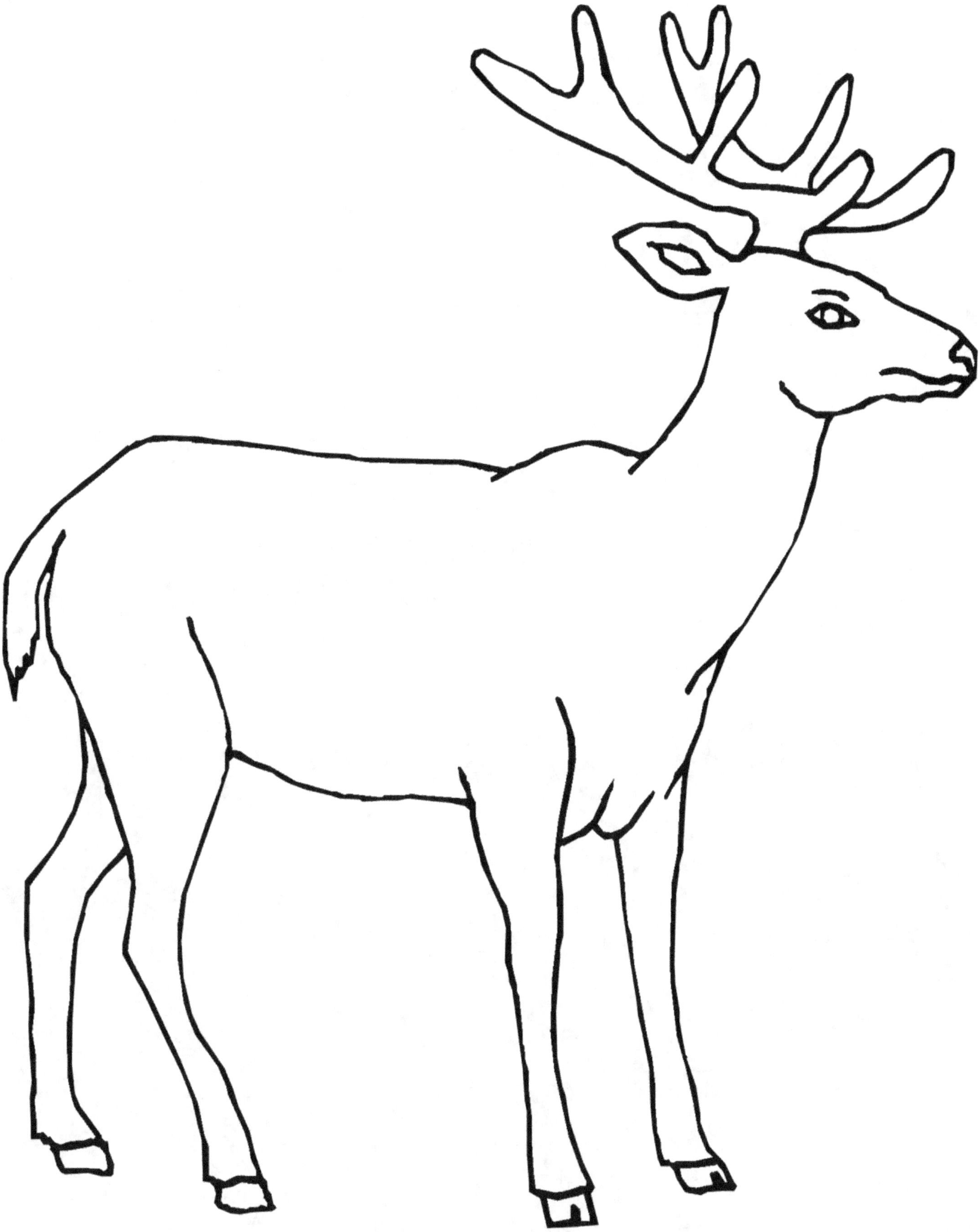

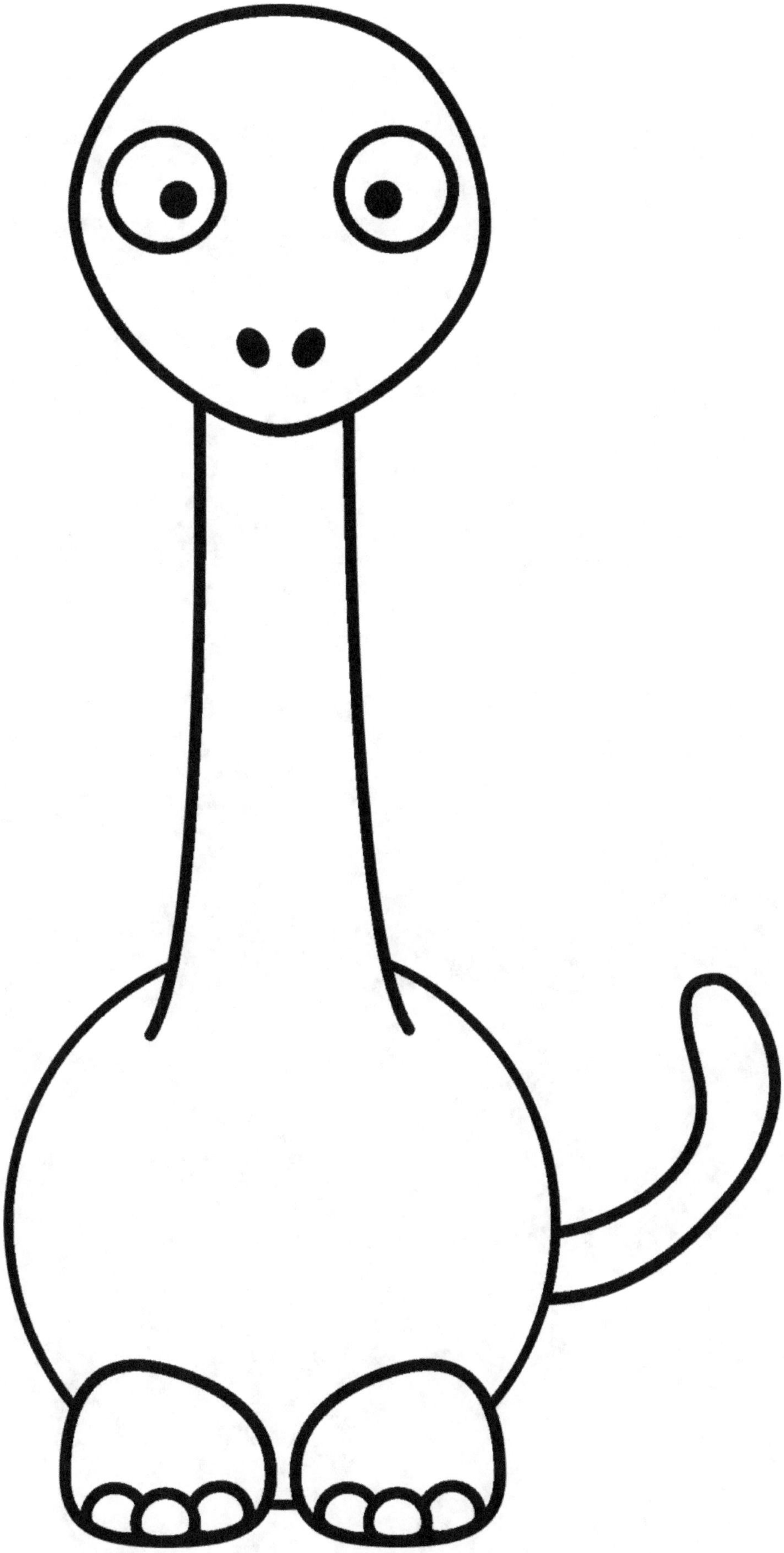

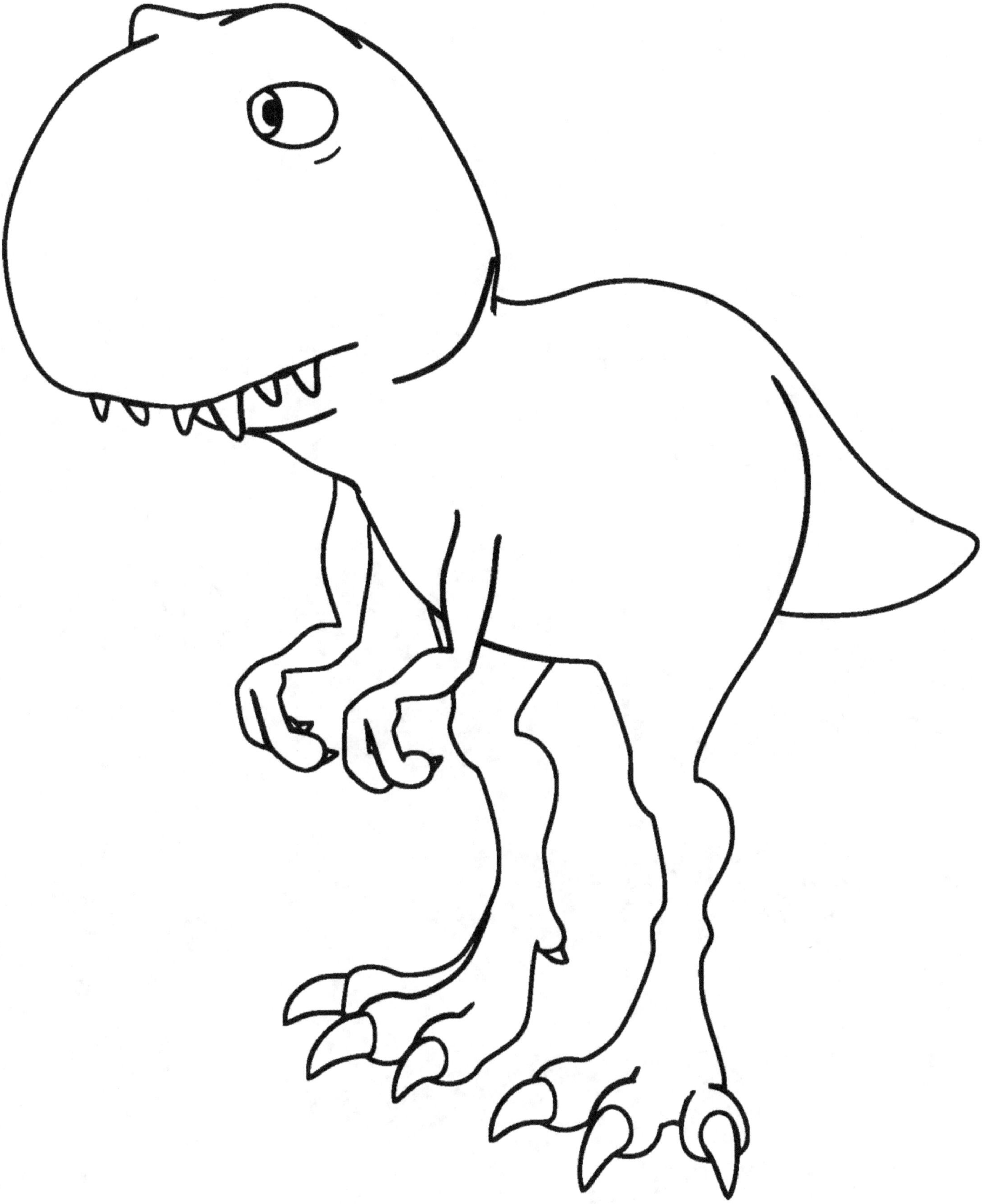

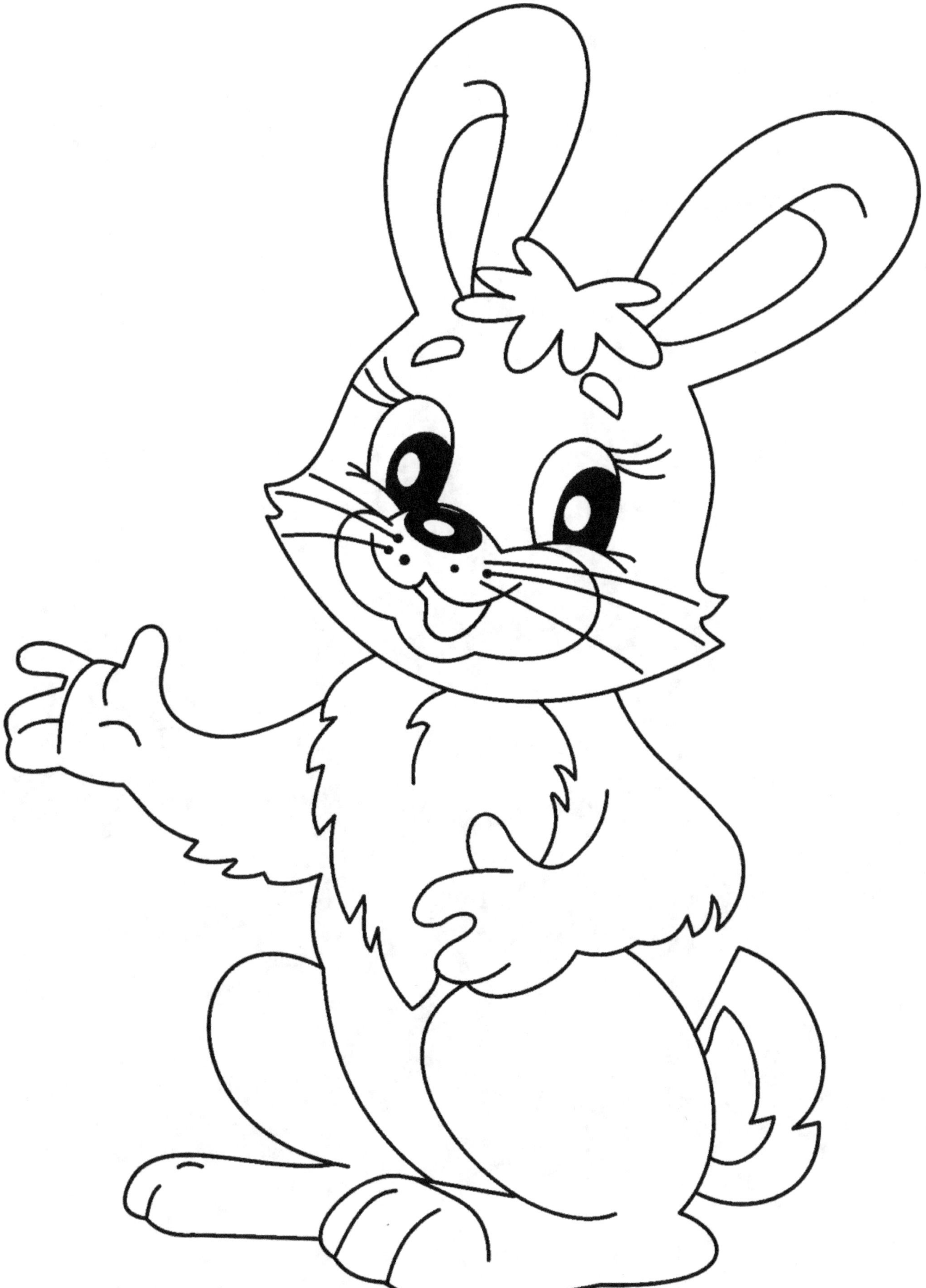

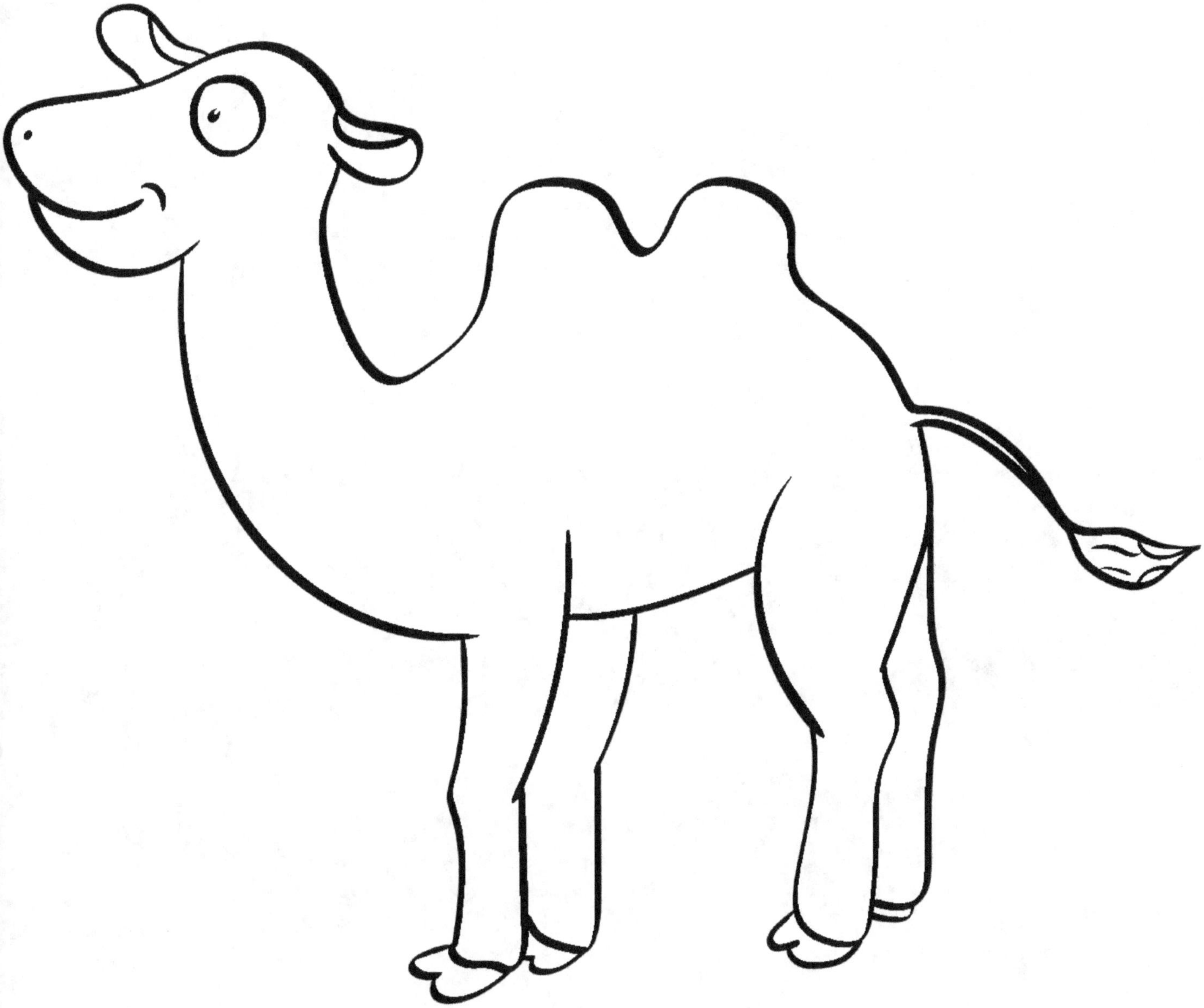

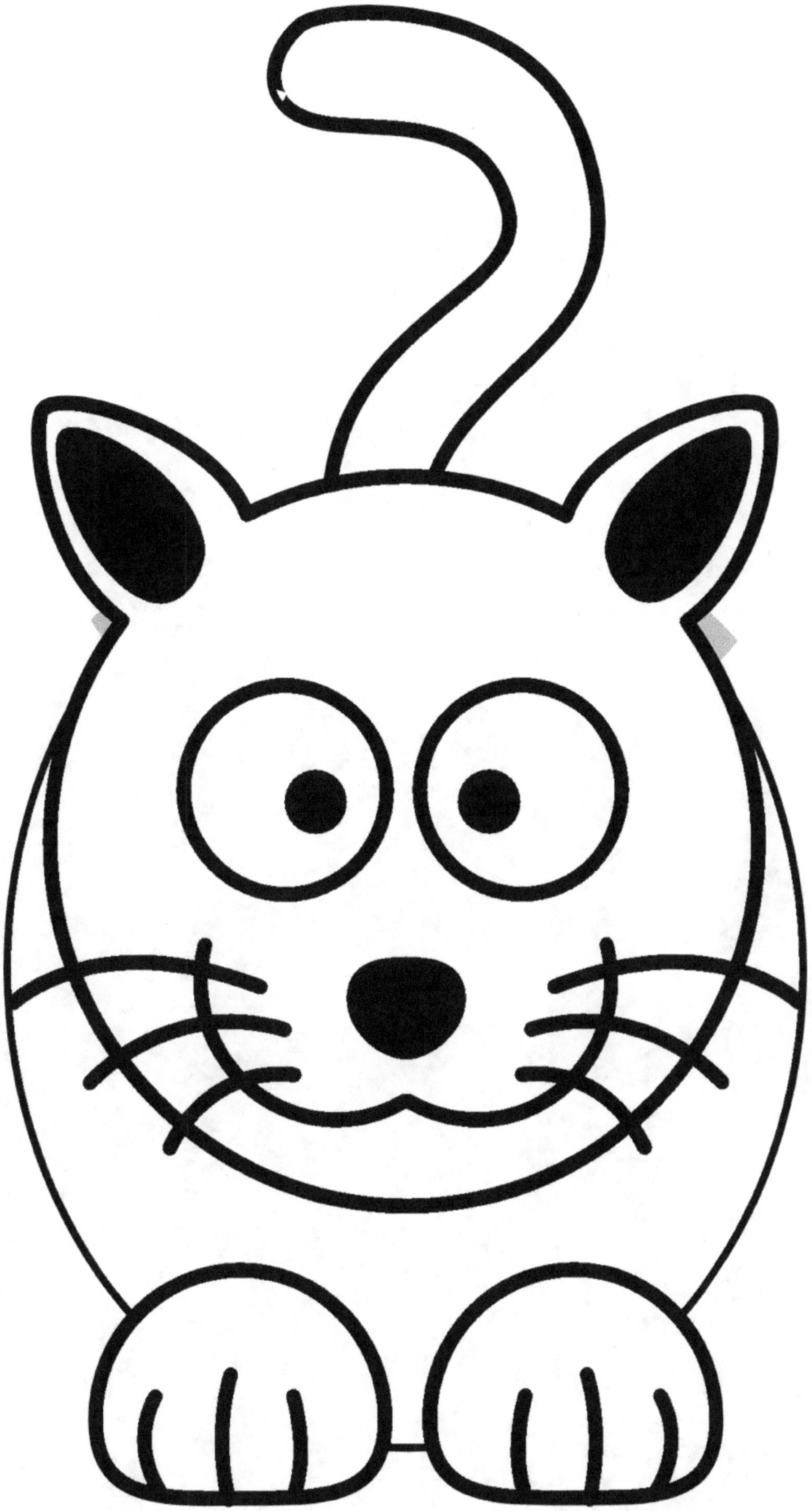

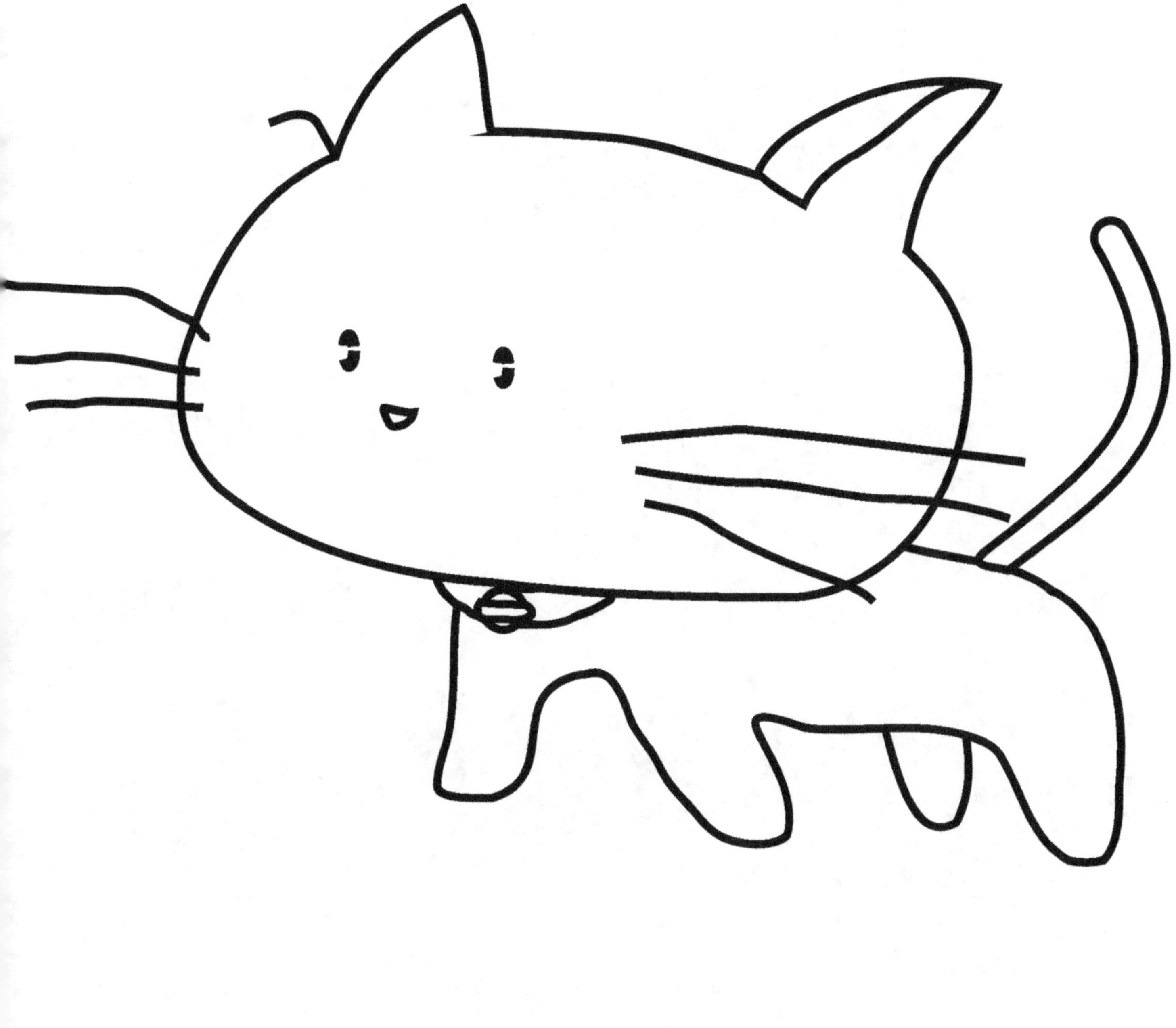

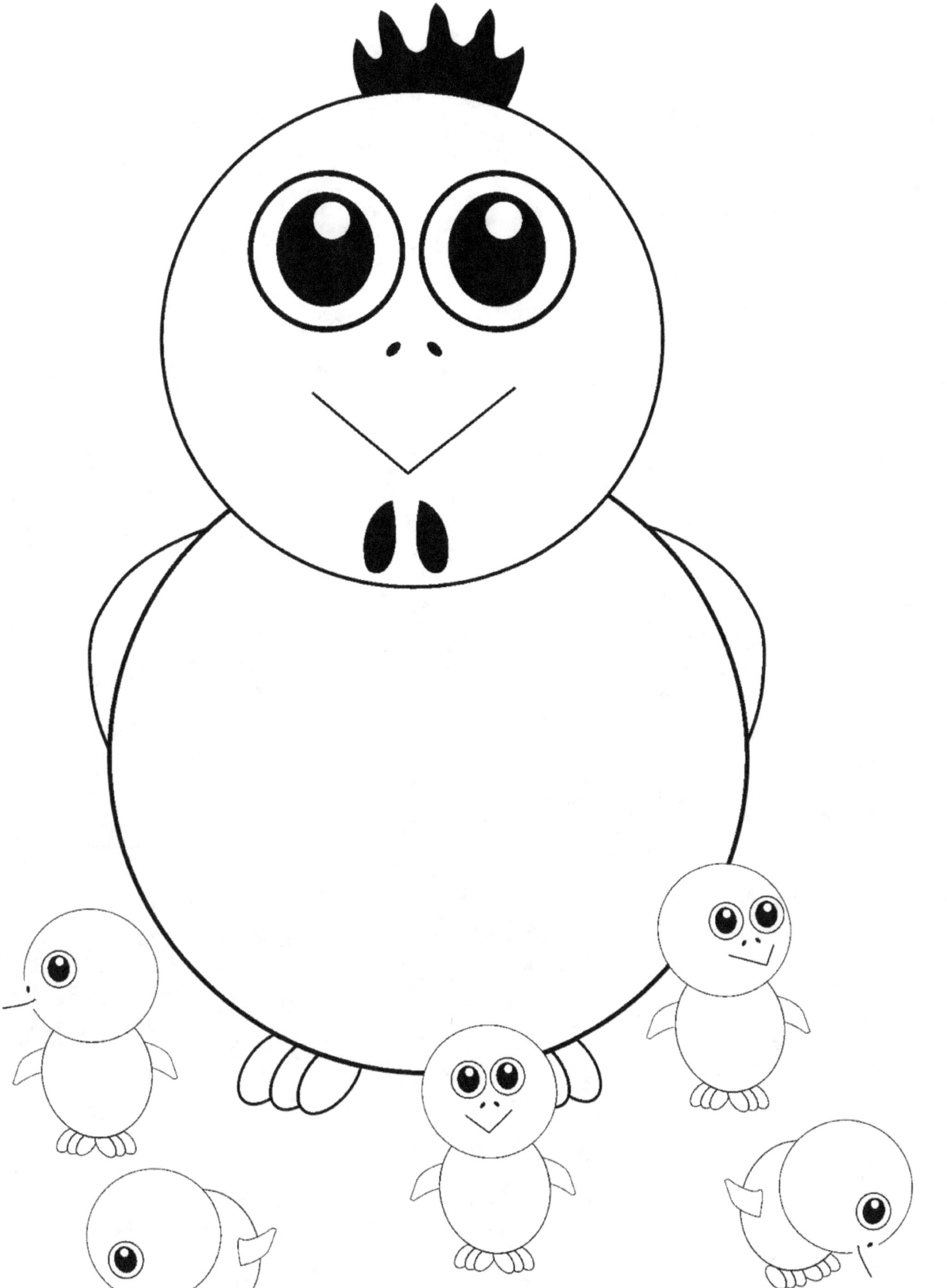

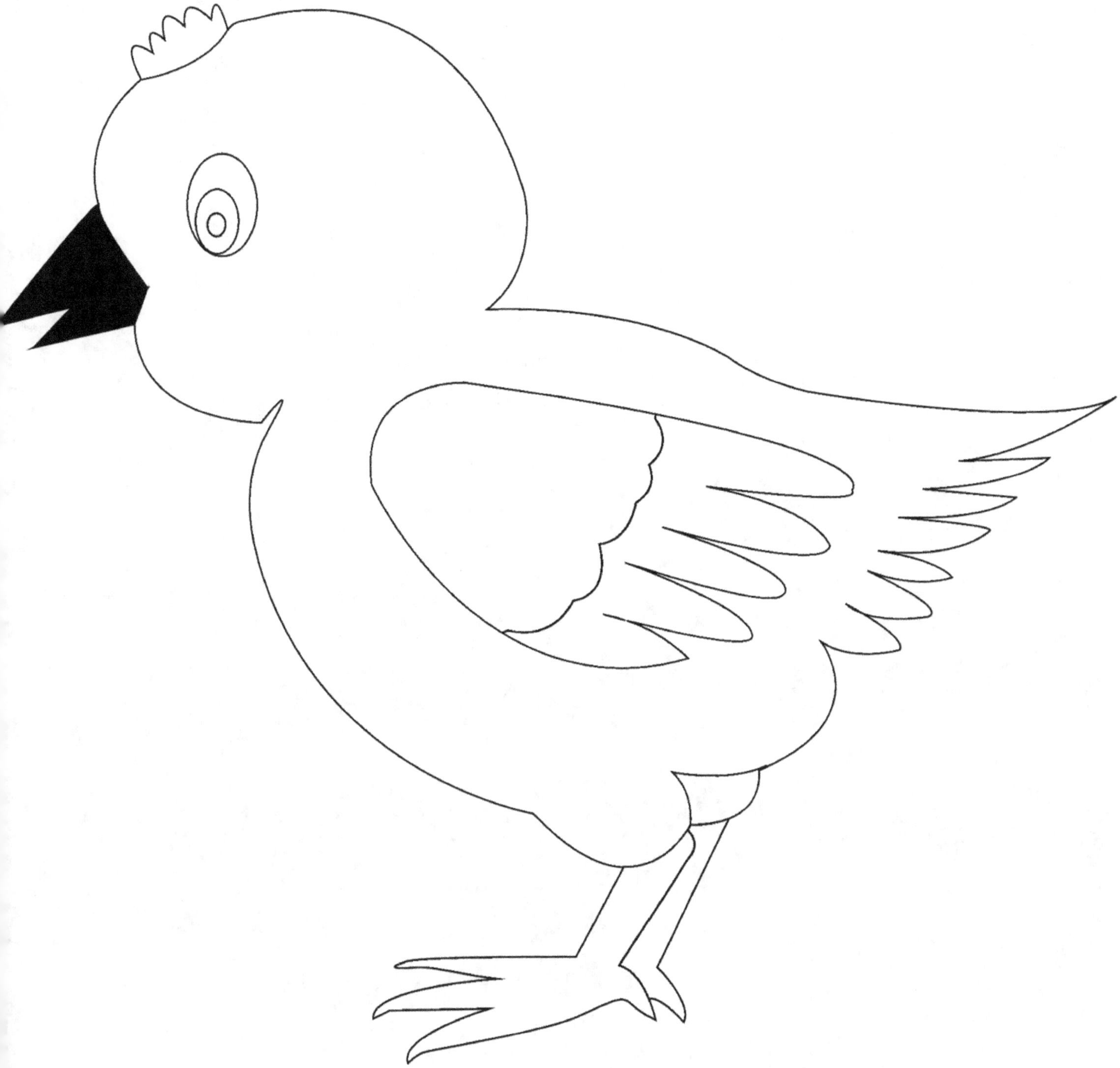

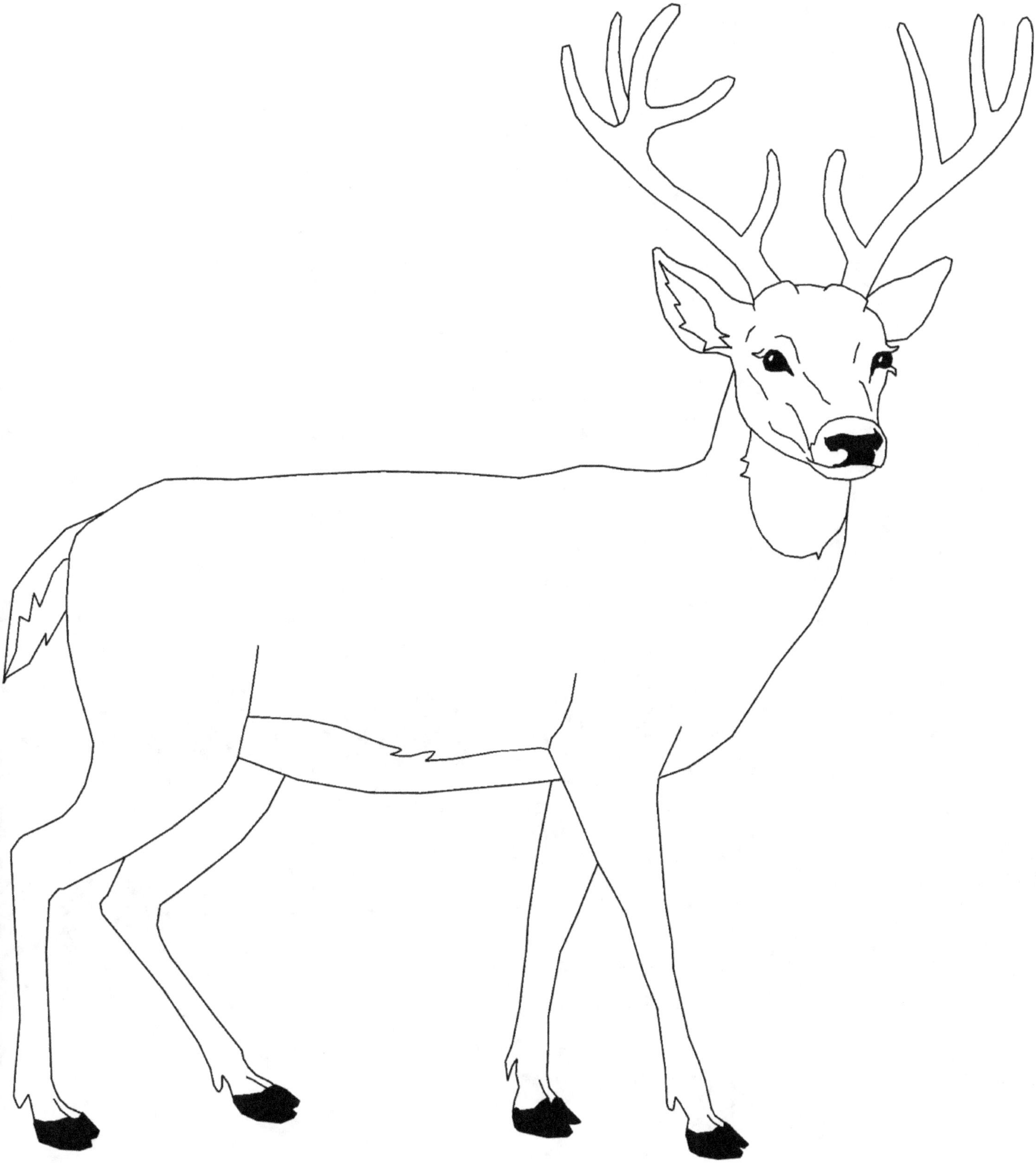

www.ingramcontent.com/pod-product-compliance
Lightning Source LLC
Chambersburg PA
CBHW080911220526
45466CB00011BA/3546
* 9 7 9 8 5 7 6 4 6 5 8 7 3 *